The Mystery of God's Providence

THE MYSTERY OF GOD'S PROVIDENCE

Paul E. Billheimer

THE STORY OF JOSEPH
GENESIS 37—50

A Television Series Broadcast
by Satellite over
Trinity Broadcasting Network

Tyndale House
Publishers, Inc.
Wheaton, Illinois

My thanks to:
Judy Alsop and Norma Aspin for many hours
of transcribing; Maria Kearns for valuable editorial
assistance; and John Rimer for manuscript reproduction.

First printing, January 1983

Library of Congress Catalog Card Number 82-62072
ISBN 0-8423-4664-3, paper
Copyright © 1983 by Paul E. Billheimer
All rights reserved
Printed in the United States of America

Norma was reared in the Catholic faith. So far as she knows, there had never been a Bible in the home for generations. She had never regularly attended mass in her adult life.

When Brad was but a baby, his father became a hopeless alcoholic and was mentally ill as a result. This forced Norma to support and rear her son alone. Life was not kind to her. She endured many cruel and severe hardships through the years.

During the summer of 1977, she "accidentally" flipped her TV dial to TBN, channel 40, and saw an elderly couple teaching from a book, *Don't Waste Your Sorrows*. Sorrows! What is valuable about sorrows? She had plenty of them. But the things they were saying spoke to her heart and aroused a great hunger to know more of what they were talking about. She did the most absurd thing of her life—she wrote to a religious telecaster asking for an appointment.

During that memorable interview, both Norma and Brad heard the way of salvation explained, step by step, until they learned how to confess their sins, repent, and receive forgiveness from the Lord Jesus Christ. Both of them experienced a glorious new birth right there in our living room. Their joy knew no bounds.

From that night forward, they simply clung to us. They returned again and again to ask questions and to receive new instructions; we coached them concerning their Bible reading and personal prayer life. Everything was new to them, but they were "walking inches off the ground." They were, indeed, "in heavenly places."

That was five years ago. Since that time they have made themselves our servants for Jesus' sake. They have truly become "our family" and look after us as though we were their very own parents. We could not carry on the ministry which the Lord has given us except for the loving assistance they provide both in our domestic needs and also in many hours of manuscript typing.

Brad was fourteen years of age when he and his mother found Jesus. As he grew older and matured more in his walk with the Lord, he received a great burden for his father's salvation. A search for his father led to a shabby "nursing home" in the slum area.

Brad regularly visited his father, explaining the way of salvation. One day, he had the joy of leading his father to Jesus and helping him to repent and receive forgiveness. When the time came for Brad and Norma to be baptized, Brad's father insisted upon joining them. He gave much evidence of real sorrow for sin. Some time later, when Brad and his mother went to the home to deliver a Christmas gift, they found him dying. He no longer knew anyone. How thankful they were to have found him and to have led him to Jesus.

Very early in the year 1980, Norma's mother went to be with the Lord. Several months before this glorious home-going, Norma had the great joy of leading her mother in the prayer of repentance, and her mother then rested her faith in Him. At the time of her passing, she rallied from a period during which she did not know her family, opened her eyes, and recognized them; then, looking above their heads, she said, "I think I am going now. Don't worry. Everything is all right." She closed her eyes and was gone—with Him.

At this writing, Norma and Brad continue their invaluable service to us, to the Lord, and to His Body.

CONTENTS

FOREWORD

I was delighted to be invited to prepare the Foreword for this message on the life of Joseph by my dear friend and brother, Paul E. Billheimer. To my mind, this man's pen is so anointed by the Holy Spirit that it *engraves* the truth of God on men's hearts.

This book has to do with an Israeli lad who went from dying in the bottom of a well pit in Dothan to become the Prime Minister of Egypt. But watch and see what our brother does with this story. In a manner too realistic for comfort, he takes Joseph's shoes from off his feet and puts them on the feet of the reader. When you begin looking at your trials, "wearing Joseph's shoes"—it does something to your spirit. Your attitude toward trials and testing undergoes a great transformation.

I loved the book. I found myself asking the Lord to get it into the hands of every Christian who will respond to it, making changes in his attitude toward the things that God allows in his life.

I also found myself thinking of the awful days that

exist even now for the suffering Church behind the Iron and Bamboo Curtains, testings that may come to us before the Lord returns. Many of us may be falsely accused and, as a result, be thrown into prison. In such a case, we may be tempted to feel that returning good for evil just doesn't work.

Ah, if we are "wearing Joseph's shoes," we will see that it does work. No matter how dark the present may appear, the Lord is in complete command of the situation. His timing is different from ours because we want relief right now.

When we finally learn that even in the midst of the deepest mysteries of His providences, God is in full control, nothing in this world can shake us or our faith. When we really are "wearing Joseph's shoes," we, too, will be able to say, "As for you, ye thought evil against me; but God meant it unto good" (Genesis 50:20). At last, every mystery will have become plain in the glorious light of His presence.

Dr. C. S. Lovett

PREFACE

The story of Joseph is a study in identity. Very few born-again believers understand who they are. This story suggests two basic theses which illuminate the question.

Amy Carmichael says that nothing anyone can do to us can injure us unless we allow it to cause a wrong reaction in our own spirits. *Only our reaction can bless or burn.* Because all reactions are subjective, they are under our control. Since the only thing that can harm us is something subject to our authority, we never need to suffer damage, no matter what others may do to us (Romans 5:17). *Therefore, every born-again person is a king and is in training for a throne.*

This brings into focus the second thesis. Because of our fabulous identity, God deals with us on the very same principles as those on which He dealt with Joseph. Since Joseph was a member of the messianic family, one who preserved, protected, and sustained it, the average Bible student assumes that he had a special identity and held a special place in God's prophetic order. In one sense this is true, *but an even greater distinction belongs to the born-again members of the family of God.* The Messiah came for one glorious purpose: to woo, win, and train the members of Christ's church *and prepare them to become His Bride.* The world, and much of the Church, does not know this, *but the universe is romantic. It was created entirely for the purpose of romance.* Joseph himself came into being for this reason. And the living and active members of the Bridehood, the actual personnel of the future Bride, are the ones who give meaning and significance to the Bride's predecessors or family. Without them, Joseph would be a blank. Therefore, each member of the Bride, now called the Church and the Body of Christ, is as fully involved in God's eternal enterprise as Joseph himself or any member of the messianic nation. *All born-again people, as members of the future Bride of Christ, are fully as significant, important, and of as great consequence in God's ongoing undertakings, adventures, and creative endeavors as any intelligence in the universe.* This is difficult to comprehend, but because God is no respecter of persons (Acts 10:34; 1 Peter 1:17), He is just as willing and anxious to do great, mighty, and supernatural things through one as through another.

God included the story of Joseph in the Bible to establish the identity of every believer. *It is a pattern of the method, manner, and technique He uses in the preparation of each member of His future Bride.* Through this biblical story God is saying to each of us, "See what I will do for you when you allow me to work unhindered in your life." God is using the same principles in preparing you for eternal rank as those He used in preparing Joseph for rulership in Egypt. Read and discover for yourself God's formula for exalted rank in the ages to come.

INTRODUCTION

Very few of us are original. Most of us are products of our past. We owe much to our heritage, our history, our culture. In the strictest sense, probably the only characters in history who can claim true originality are the authors of Holy Writ—and their originality is the result of the inspiration of the Holy Spirit. "For no prophecy recorded in Scripture was ever thought up by the prophet himself. It was the Holy Spirit within these godly men who gave them true messages from God" (2 Peter 1:20, 21, *The Living Bible*). All truth that is absolutely original is in the written Word of God because the Holy Spirit alone is the source of all truth. He is called "the Spirit of truth" (John 16:13). Therefore, no one, not even the sacred writers, can claim absolute originality.

However, in a modified and accommodated sense, all genuine truth that is communicated, quickened, made alive and real to any human spirit is original because it was authored and energized by the Holy Spirit.

I wish to give proper credit for the truths and messages which I share with you. I am deeply indebted to many sources. I owe much to the works of John Wesley, Alexander Maclaren, Stuart Holden, J. R. Miller, A. B. Simpson, Amy Carmichael, Watchman Nee, and many others. For much of the emphasis in this series, I am indebted to a book on the life of Joseph by J. R. Miller. I am grateful for the insights and some of the language gleaned from his book which, by the help of the Spirit, has been grist for my own spiritual "mill."

One of the most important and challenging theses of this study is one stated by Amy Carmichael: *Nothing anyone can do to us can injure us unless we submit to a wrong reaction.* She says that the eternal essence of a thing, a situation, or circumstance is not in the thing itself but in our reaction to it. It is not what anyone does to us that injures us but it is the way we take it, the spirit in which we react. Only our reaction can bless or burn. We may not control what other people do to us but, by God's grace, we can control our response. Since the only thing that can harm us is something under our control (i.e., our reaction), *we never need to suffer damage no matter what others may do.* This gives meaning to Romans 5:17: "For if by one man's offence death reigned by one; much more they which receive abundance of grace and of the gift of righteousness shall reign in life by one, Jesus Christ." *Since this is true, no one ever needs to be the victim of circumstances.* Every son of God is a king and may realize and demonstrate his kingship. Because by God's grace he can control his own reaction, he never needs to be subject to the whims of anyone else. He has the power, by controlling his own reaction, to cause all things to work together for his good, because when his own reaction is correct, he grows in all of the graces of the Spirit. He is blessed. He is made better.

This is the lesson which we may learn from Joseph. We will call attention to this truth many times. When, with the Spirit's help, we learn to live by this principle, we "have it made," as the saying goes. This is our aim in this study.

It is most important to remember that this truth applies, not primarily in time, but in eternity. Joseph's life proves that it is valid in time, in the present throbbing moment, *but its primary application is to the eternal sphere.* "For our light affliction, which is but for a moment, worketh for us a far more exceeding and eternal weight of glory; while we look not at the things which are seen, but at the things which are not seen: for the things which are seen are temporal; but the things which are not seen are eternal" (2 Corinthians 4:17, 18). "For I reckon that the sufferings of this present time are not worthy to be compared with the glory which shall be revealed in us" (Romans 8:18).

Both the temporal and eternal dimensions of this truth are demonstrated in the story of Joseph's life. We pray you will follow these lessons and discover for yourself many principles that you can develop and use in your own trials and circumstances.

ONE
THE MYSTERY OF
GOD'S PROVIDENCE

"Thy judgments are a great deep" (Psalm 36:6).

Because God's judgments are so full of mystery, because it is so difficult for the finite mind to fathom them, we are in danger of discounting their wisdom and even doubting the intelligence behind them. Most of us are tempted, when calamity comes, to regard it as purely accidental. Very few of us have the faith of the writer of these lines based on Romans 8:28, "All things work together for good to them that love the Lord":

> For every pain that we must bear,
> For every sorrow, every care,
>   There is a reason.
>
> For every falsehood that is said,
> For every teardrop that is shed,
>   There is a reason.

For every grief, for every trial,
For every weary, lonely mile,
  There is a reason.

But if we trust Him as we should,
All will work out for our good;
  God knows the reason.

When we can have that faith; when we can but know there is a "needs be" for each pain; when we can be convinced that there is an intelligence and a design in the circumstances of our lives, that there is indeed and in fact "a divinity that shapes our ends, rough-hew them how we will" (Shakespeare), then we can not only submit, but we can welcome joyfully, triumphantly, and victoriously whatever life brings, whether of joy or of sorrow.

MYSTERY MEANS
DEEP INTELLIGENCE AND DESIGN
Mystery! Think of it for a moment. What is mystery? Mystery does not mean absence of design. Mystery does not mean the lack of intelligence. *It means that the design is deep, profound, hidden.* Even though we cannot see it, the plot is there; the purpose is there; intelligence is there. It may be intelligence that transcends our power to discover and discern, but it is there. *Mystery does not mean that motive is absent.* It only means that it is more vast, boundless, and significant. Isn't that the reason that mystery is so fascinating? A mystery story, a mystery play—that is what makes it a thriller, the mystery in it.

I wonder if we looked at the mystery of life—at the mystery of God's dealings with us from that angle—

our lives would not have more thrill in them. That is the reason mystery is so fascinating. *It is because there is an intelligent plot and a comprehensive plan that contains many facets, has many threads.* It is so deep, so well thought out, that for the time being we are unable to fathom any design, any understandable purpose. We know that underneath, something is going on which later will become plain.

DEEP MYSTERY MEANS A GREAT PLOT

Where there is no mystery, there is no plot. *Deep mystery means a great plot. A great mind is behind it.* This is especially true with mysteries of a life that is yielded to God. This is what the Psalmist meant when he said in Psalm 36:6: "Thy judgments are a great deep." He had reference to God's dealings with His people. Not many of us can discern it but *God has a pattern, a plan, a blueprint by which He works in every life.* Nobody is left out. Because that plot, that plan, or that blueprint is so great, so deep, so involved, so intricate and far-reaching, it is hard to understand. It is difficult to fathom. We cannot see through it. Because we cannot see through it, because it is so complicated, so minutely detailed, and because it covers such a vast expanse, we are in danger of deciding there is no plot at all. Yet, beloved, much thought has gone into God's plan, and God's blueprint, and God's prototype for your life and mine. *Infinite intelligence drew that plan and not one detail was overlooked.* It requires training and skill to read any blueprint. Not only does it require training and skill, including years of preparation, it also requires education, practice, and faith to read and understand God's blueprints. Only those who are skilled in faith, who believe in the supernatural, are able to discern the plot in God's dealings with His people. Those who lack this discernment see no purpose, no motive, no intelligence in the course of human events. But those whose eyes have been quickened by faith can understand and say with confidence:

> *Behind my life the Weaver stands;*
>   *And works His wondrous will.*
> *I leave it in His all-wise hands,*
>   *And trust His perfect skill.*
> *Should mystery enshroud His plan,*
>   *And my short sight be dimmed,*
> *I will not try the whole to scan,*
>   *But leave each thread with Him.*

UNFINISHED PLANS CREATE MYSTERY

One of the mysteries of God's dealings with us is that we do not yet see the completed picture, the finished plan. *The plot of a story may not become clear until the end of the book.* We have to read the last chapter, the last page, sometimes the very last sentence, before we can understand the motive. Just so it is in God's dealings with us. We cannot see the reason, we cannot comprehend and fathom the plot and the mystery *because we have not read far enough.* Let us not make hasty judgments, beloved, for God is not yet through. The book is not yet finished.

THE INCOMPLETE PICTURE

Most of us have watched a chalk artist draw a picture. It may be a landscape or a character sketch. Have you ever noticed how meaningless it is in the beginning? He makes a number of marks or unsightly blots upon the paper. We cannot yet see any design or any plan in the picture. We do not see any reason or any meaning. There is nothing attractive, and if we have never watched him before we may have a feeling of disappointment. Various shapes and colors are thrown upon the easel, apparently without discrimination. It makes no sense. There is no beauty, no coordination. But as we watch, the plot thickens—a mark here, a dash of color there, a stroke here or there—and gradually a motif begins to appear. Maybe just one little twist of the chalk gives the first clue, possibly only a dot and, presto, the plan unfolds. When the picture is completed we see that there was a reason for every little mark and every little dash of color, that it all fits into the plan that was in the mind of the artist in the beginning. What seemed like meaningless "chicken tracks" at first, we now discover were a part of a gorgeous sunset or a beautiful face. So it is with God's plans and judgments. As the Psalmist said, "Thy judgments are a great deep." They are full of mystery because the picture is incomplete. The story has not yet been finished.

AN INTEGRAL PART OF THE DIVINE PLAN
This has been clearly illustrated in the life of Joseph. *Let us not think that God dealt with Joseph on the basis of any peculiar principle.* Not everyone believes this, but God is no respecter of persons (Acts 10:34; 1 Peter 1:17), and the principles by which He dealt with Joseph so long ago are the same as those by which He deals with us all. You may find this difficult to accept but it is basic to the understanding of the story. *We are all an integral part of God's plan for the ages.* We may think today that our spiritual circumstances are so limited that the

principles God used in dealing with Joseph have no application whatever to the circumstances of our lives. *That is a fatal mistake.* It is the result of our failure to understand our identity as a member of the Body and Bride of Christ.

TWO
ULTIMATE GOAL
OF THE UNIVERSE

Perhaps you are one who doubts that God deals with us today on the same principles upon which He dealt with Joseph so long ago. An unknown poet has said: "Through the ages one eternal purpose runs." Although these are not the words of Scripture, they define an important scriptural law. As revealed in the closing chapters of Revelation, *the ultimate goal of the universe is the Church, later to be the Bride, united and reigning with Christ.* All events of biblical history which precede the glorious climax of the ages are occupied with and directed toward that one end. There are various stages of development but the enterprise is one unified whole. From the creation of the universe to the eternal ages, the goal of all of God's aims, purposes, and actions is one—only one: *the selection and preparation of an eternal companion for the Son.* This is the only biblical or rational explanation of existence. It follows, therefore, that every single operation, project, or event which occurs at any stage of development and which contributes to the ultimate goal is an intrinsic part and parcel of the same process. All work that contributes to the same end is the same sort of work.

Joseph, Moses, Samuel, and the Prophets made contributions to the eternal project in the initial or early stages of the program. That project was the preparation and development of the messianic nation through whom the Messiah came. The Messiah came for one and only one purpose: to give birth to His Church, thus to obtain His Bride. The Church age marks the consummation of God's plan to select and train the members of His Bridehood. *Therefore, this present age and its participants cannot be less important than the preceding stages.*

SEEING YOUR FACE IN THIS MIRROR

This is the basis for the statement that God deals with those who form the ultimate goal and constitute the final object of His eternal purpose upon the same principles upon which He dealt with Joseph. This is God's way of telling us that His relationship with us is personal, individualistic, intimate, and exclusive and is just as authentically relevant as it is with all others of any day or age in history. Some who believe that Jesus is the same, still believe that the day of miracles is past and that God's supernatural acts recorded in the Bible have only historical significance. These people do not deny the truth of the Word but they interpret it as relevant only to the past. Others believe that "through the ages one eternal purpose runs" and all that God ever did in any age He is just as able, willing, and committed to do today. They believe that all of His mighty acts recorded in the Word are there as examples of the way He works in every age when faith is present. This is what they mean by claiming that Jesus is the same yesterday, today, and forever.

"For whatsoever things were written aforetime were written for our learning, that we through patience and comfort of the scriptures might have hope" (Romans 15:4). No one has to believe anything I say to keep on good terms with me, but when you believe this, you will be able to put yourself in Joseph's place and to see your face in this mirror. Many believe that in every age, *God meets us on the highest spiritual level on which we can meet Him.*

Would God have given space in His Word to the story of Joseph merely as history? According to 1 Corinthians 10:11 we who constitute the Church are those "upon whom the fulfillment of the ages has come" (NIV). I believe this present generation is engaged in the final fulfillment of God's vision and purpose. *Therefore, the principles by which He dealt with Joseph are in no sense obsolete or outdated.* If so, He deals with us on these same eternal principles.

SEE WHAT I WILL DO FOR YOU
Therefore, let us remember this: God put the story of Joseph in the Bible, among other things, for the purpose of teaching us how He deals with us when we work with Him as Joseph did. God is saying through Joseph's life, "See what I will do for you if you will yield to me as Joseph did and if you will take things that come to you as Joseph took the things that came to him." *Beloved, if the principles that God used in dealing with Joseph are the very same that He uses in dealing with us, He will do similar things for us, provided we allow Him.* The only reason we understand God's dealings with such

men as Joseph and Job is that we have before us the completed picture, the finished story. By studying God's dealings with these men, we can see that every little detail was planned and had its place. We can see plainly a definite design, but we can see it only because we have the whole story before us. Remember that Joseph and Job could not see the plan when they were in the midst of their suffering and distress, because the "picture" was not finished. To them it was just like the chalk picture we were talking about a moment ago.

God is telling us through these recorded experiences that He is working with us in the same way and that when the whole story is complete, we shall see the meaning of each portion of the plan which now seems so mysterious to us, and we shall approve it all. *We will look back and see that we could not have afforded to miss even one little part of the plan.* As Anna Shipton has said concerning David, "One thrill of anguish and fear; one blessing unmarked or unpriced; one difficulty or danger evaded: How great would have been our loss in that thrilling psalmody in which God's people today find the expression of their grief or of their praise."

THE UNFOLDING OF THE MYSTERY

It is a mystery now. We cannot understand it. *Our lives do not make sense to us.* This thing through which we are passing, this sorrow, this disappointment, the perfidy of traitorous friends, the deception of people around us, the cruelty that seems to come so undeserved—all of this is a part of a plot that is grandly conceived and brilliantly implemented. It hurts. It pains us. It is just like one of those dark blots that was placed on the picture which we watched. First it is ugly, but when the picture is completed it stands out in beauty and splendor. Without it something would have been missing, something would have been lacking. So the poet has said:

> Not till the loom is silent, and the shuttles cease to fly,
> Shall God unfold the pattern and explain the reason why
> The dark threads were as needful in the Master's skillful hand
> As the threads of gold and silver in the pattern which He planned.

I know it is difficult for us now to see that there is any plan, any reason, any justification for the hurt and the sorrow, for the disappointment, for the grief; but God, the great Master-Painter, knows what He is doing, and when it is finished, we shall see there was a "needs be" for every part of the picture.

THREE
THE WORD OF GOD RATHER THAN A HOROSCOPE

We may understand better the mystery that enshrouds God's providences and dealings with us as we see in the life of Joseph the *why* of that mystery in his life. Why is it that God keeps things from us? How often we would like to pull aside the curtain and look down into the future, so that we might choose our own way and avoid the rough paths. As we study the life of Joseph, we see one of the reasons why God hides so much of the future from us.

One of the reasons some go to clairvoyant specialists such as fortune tellers, palm readers, and mediums is that we think if we knew the future, we could make our own decisions and use our own judgment instead of trusting God's guidance and wisdom. Genuine faith in God would enable us to say with the songwriter, "I may not know the way I go, but O! I know my guide." Beware of putting your faith in such uncertain portents as seers, mediums, and stargazers. *The Word of God, not your horoscope, has the divinely inspired answer to questions.*

THE BLESSING OF NOT KNOWING

Suppose Joseph had been told, on his way to Dothan, how his brothers would treat him—that he was to be placed in a pit and later sold as a slave into Egypt. Do you think he would have gone on? Would you have gone on under those conditions and circumstances? I think most of us would have turned back, and I think perhaps Joseph would have turned back. If Joseph had been told what was going to take place at Dothan and he *had* turned back, how different the story would have been. Joseph would have lost all the bright future which lay beyond the cruel treatment. Think also what Joseph's family would have lost and furthermore what the world would have missed.

Dr. J. R. Miller, in his little book on the story of Joseph, has said, "It would not be well for us to know what is before us. We would often meddle with God's plans and spoil them, marring our own future and harming others. *Nothing can really go wrong with us if He is leading us and we are quietly following Him.* Though He takes us through pain, misfortune, and suffering, it is because that is the path to true blessing and good."

HUMAN SHORTSIGHTEDNESS

Someone has tried to imagine how different Joseph's life story could have been and has tried to illustrate it like this: Let us suppose someone outside of our universe was looking down upon the Hebrew lad in the hands of the Midianites. Joseph, being an active and ingenious lad, escaped from the caravan the first night after his brothers had sold him. He had just reached the outer edge of the camp when a dog began to bark and awakened the men who were in charge of him, and he was returned to captivity.

34

However, the person looking on from outside our universe, according to this imaginary story, wanted to kill the dog before he had awakened the camp. In that case Joseph would have gotten away and would have reached home in safety. Great sorrow would have been avoided on Joseph's part. But when the man who was looking on wanted to kill the dog, the guardian angel stood there and would not permit him, saying, "Hands off!" In order to let him see the evil of interference, the guardian angel took the man into a world where he could try the experiment and see its results. There the dog was killed and Joseph reached home in safety. His father rejoiced and his brothers were comforted. It certainly seemed a better way than the other. But when the famine came there was no Joseph in Egypt to foretell it and to prepare for it. There was no food laid up in the storehouses. Palestine and Egypt were devastated by starvation. Great numbers died and the savage Hittites destroyed those whom the famine had spared. Civilization was set back centuries. Egypt was blotted out. Greece and Rome remained in a barbarous state. The history of the whole world was changed and countless evils came; all because a man in his ignorance killed a dog, saving a boy from present trouble to his own and the world's great future loss. Dr. Miller says, "We would better keep our hands off God's providences. Many a beautiful plan of His is spoiled by human meddling."

IF WE COULD SEE BEYOND TODAY
Peter wanted to keep Jesus away from the Cross. Of course we know he couldn't, but suppose he had done so—what would have been the result? No doubt, many a time shortsighted love has kept a life from

hardship, sacrifice, and suffering, thereby blighting or marring a destiny, a plan of God.

We are likely to pity the boy Joseph as we see him enter this period of humiliation by being sold as a slave and then cast into irons. We see, if human pity could have rescued him from the sad part of his life, that the glorious part that followed would have been lost. Few truths are more sustaining to Christian faith than this—*that our times are in God's hands.* We forget it too often. When life brings hard things to endure, when our own plans are broken, sometimes we fret, but someday we shall see that God knew best.

> *If we could see beyond today, as God can see,*
> *If all the clouds could roll away, the shadows flee,*
> *For present griefs we would not fret;*
> *Each sorrow we should soon forget,*
> *For many joys are waiting yet,*
>   *For you and me.*
>
> *If we could know beyond today, as God doth know,*
> *Why dearest treasures pass away, and tears must flow,*
> *And why the darkness leads to light,*
> *Why dreary paths would soon grow bright;*
> *Some day life's wrongs will be made right;*
>   *Faith tells us so.*
>
> *If we could see, if we could know, we often say:*
> *But God, in love, a veil doth throw across our way;*
> *We cannot see what lies before,*
> *And so we cling to Him the more;*
> *He leads us till this life is o'er;*
>   *Trust and obey.*

Author Unknown

FOUR
A "NEEDS BE" FOR PAIN

We are going to see, as the poet has said, that there is a "needs be" for each pain and each difficulty in Joseph's life. *God is thereby trying to teach us that there is likewise a "needs be" for many unwelcome things which come into our lives.* He is saying that if we meet them in the same spirit in which Joseph met his, God will work for us in the same way as He worked for Joseph. The great victory that Joseph obtained was that he came through his difficulty, his thirteen years of humiliation, unhurt. Because his reaction was right, he came out without yielding to the temptation to bitterness, which would have destroyed God's plan for him and the Hebrew race.

Think of the sense of wrong which must have filled his heart as he remembered the treatment he received from his brothers. They had torn him away from his home; they had been about to kill him; they had sold him as a slave. Surely it was difficult to keep a heart sweet and free from resentment with such a consciousness of injustice in the soul. It is difficult to

37

conceive of a condition more discouraging. It was a sore test of character to which Joseph was exposed. The treatment he had received from his brothers would make almost anyone vengeful. The circumstances would be enough to crush very nearly any spirit.

THE ONLY INJURY

There are few men who pass through such experiences of injustice and cruelty as those Joseph met, and still keep their hearts sweet and gentle, their faith in God bright and clear, their spirits brave and strong. It showed the healthiness and wholesomeness of Joseph's nature as he passed through the galling and trying experiences with his spirit unhurt. He was kept from being soured toward people. He did not grow morbid, sullen, or disheartened. Though a slave, he accepted his position with cheerfulness and entered heartily into his new life, doing his duty so well that he soon became overseer in his master's house. He wasted no time or strength in weeping over his misfortune or plotting revenge. He did not grieve over his wrongs nor debase himself by self-pity.

One of the most miserable and unmanly emotions one can entertain is self-pity. He did not burn out the love of his heart in vindictive and resentful feeling. He did not brood over his wrongs. He looked forward and not back. These are the things that injure the spirit and the spirit is the real person. If your spirit takes no injury, then you yourself are not injured. What God is telling us in the story of Joseph is that we are not actually subject to any human personality or set of circumstances. "Who is he that will harm you, if ye be followers of that which is good?" (1 Peter 3:13), that is, if you are victorious in your spirit and your reaction. "Let your conversation be without covetousness; and be content with such things as ye have: for he hath said, I will never leave thee, nor forsake thee. So that we may boldly say, the Lord is my helper, and I will not fear what man shall do unto me" (Hebrews 13:5, 6). *Only what injures our spirit actually injures us.*

THE WILL IS THE MAN
Perhaps someone is saying, "I can't help the way I feel. When people wrong me, how can I control my reaction?" Mrs. Hannah Whitehall Smith, in her little book *The Christian's Secret of a Happy Life,* has given us the secret. She says that the "will" is the man; that is, the "will," not the emotions, is the fundamental identifying essence of the person or personality. When you are first wronged you may not be able easily to control your emotions, but everyone, unless he is demon possessed, is able to control his will. When you suffer injustice, your emotions may react, but if you "will" to "will" God's will, then your reaction is correct no matter how you feel. If you continue to "will" God's will, which is always to forgive, eventually your emotions will harmonize with your will. *That is victory.* This apparently was the way Joseph controlled his reaction.

"NOT WHAT OTHERS DO"
This, beloved, is one of the secrets of Joseph's final exaltation. With hatred all about him, he kept love in his heart. In the midst of injuries, wrongs, and injustices, *his spirit was forgiving.* Unforgiveness, resentment, holding a grudge, all are self-destructive. With a thousand things that tended to discourage and dis-

hearten him, to break his spirit, still he refused to be discouraged. *The fact that other men lived unworthily was but a stronger reason why he should live honorably.* That he was treated cruelly and wickedly was fresh reason why he should give to others about him the best service of love and unselfishness. That his condition was hard was to him a new motive for living heroically and nobly. *Joseph is thus preaching to us that it is not what others do to us that injures us, but only our reaction to it.* Let us not miss the lesson.

ONLY A WRONG REACTION

In a word, we are to live victoriously, truly, nobly, sweetly, cheerfully, songfully, in spite of whatever may be uncongenial in our condition *because only a wrong reaction can do us permanent harm.* Without forgiveness, Joseph would have been totally disqualified for the duties of rulership. No one can lord it over a person who has learned to control his reaction to injustice. He is a king.

At that early period, in some supernatural way, God had illuminated Joseph's spirit and convinced him that because God is Love, agape love is the most powerful force in the universe. Even today, with the full illumination of the gospel, not all of us have discovered this. *This is the secret God is telling us through the story of Joseph.*

FIVE
A RIGHT REACTION

In an effort to discover the key to God's dealings with us we continue our study of the mystery of God's providence as revealed in the life of Joseph. As we have said, God is preaching to us through the record of His dealings with Joseph. We believe that God is the same yesterday, today, and forever and that there is no respect of persons with Him. *Therefore, in God's providential dealings in Joseph's life may be found the key to the principles by which He deals with us.*

SILENCE UNDER FALSE ACCUSATION

Let us notice some of the important principles exhibited in Joseph's life. Take, for instance, his *silence under false accusation.* Here is a real test of character. Not many of us are up to this standard but it seems that Joseph went to prison without telling Potiphar any of the facts of the case. Joseph's temptress, in her disappointment and anger, charged him with most dishonorable behavior. Under this accusation, Joseph was seized and cast into prison, but there is no evidence that he said one word to Potiphar to turn suspicion upon his accusing wife. He seems to have thought of protecting Potiphar's home and position. Rather than lay a stain upon it, he would go to the dungeon under false charges, leaving to God the vindication of his own honor and the proving of his own innocence.

Beloved, God is here preaching to us. He sets forth this principle of silence under false accusation as one of the standards of integrity which He values most highly and which He must see developed in the life of the man that He honors. It has been said, "For his purity, you will find his equal one among a thousand (speaking of Joseph); for his mercy, scarcely one." By a word he could have told Potiphar the whole story, but apparently rather than speak that word, he allowed the dishonoring accusations to rest undenied. Nothing is harder than to live under false charges which bring upon one suspicion and condemnation and which, by breaking silence, one could cast off. There are persons who do live thus, bearing reproach and odium to shield others. Joseph had resisted temptation in order to be loyal to Potiphar. Now Potiphar thinks him guilty of the very baseness which, for love of him, he had scorned to commit. *Yet in all of this, Joseph's apparent confidence that the universe was under God's benevolent control and that agape love is the most powerful force extant—this enabled him to keep his heart sweet and loving.*

THE SECRET OF JOSEPH'S EXALTATION
Here is the secret of Joseph's final exaltation: a right reaction. It was the fact that he kept sweet. *He did not grow bitter.* This is the real battle of all life, beloved: to keep the heart loving, to keep resentment out of the

spirit, to keep a right reaction in the unfortunate experiences of life.

Not everyone knows this, but yielding to a wrong spirit binds the hands of the Holy Spirit and prevents His benevolent operation in one's behalf. It always injures the person harboring the wrong spirit more than its object. Joseph lay now in a dungeon. Perhaps many would look at Joseph and think he was a fool. The average man of the world, not knowing what was coming out of this, even today, would call Joseph a fool. But Joseph did not take things out of God's hands. Evidently he believed that God is in control and that as the Psalmist said, "My times are in thy hand" (Psalms 31:15). What a comfort it is to know that "He [Jesus] regulates the universe by the mighty power of his command" (Hebrews 1:3 *The Living Bible*) and that all things, both good and apparently evil, are working together for the good of those who love the Lord (Romans 8:28). What a joy to know that nothing can come to a child of God without His permission and that almighty love never permits anything that is not for the good of the loved one. Do all of us who profess to be Spirit-filled live by this faith?

THE TEMPTATION OF ILLICIT SEX
Here is another thought which has been suggested. *Joseph's loss through doing right was nothing in comparison with what he would have lost had he done the wickedness to which he was tempted.* What would have happened if Joseph had yielded to temptation and had connived with Potiphar's wife? I know that some would have thought that was a way of getting Joseph out of his slavery, but sin always has a way of finding us out and it would have found Joseph out (Numbers 32:23).

According to Proverbs 6:32, 33, the sin of adultery is self-destructive; that is, it produces a permanent, irrecoverable injury. "A man who commits adultery lacks judgment; whoever does so destroys himself. Blows and disgrace are his lot; and his shame will never be wiped away."

Joseph was living in a cesspool of iniquity. This temptation was Satan's way of ruining him and defeating God's plan for the nurture of the messianic nation. Satan sought then to use sex sin to defeat God's ultimate goal in the creation of the universe to select and train an eternal companion for the Son. Today it may be that the greatest threat to obtaining that goal is the same—illicit sex. Many believe that Hollywood is Satan's most notorious ally and his most successful instrument in corrupting the world and staining and tarnishing the Bride.

It has been said that Joseph's prison gloom, deep as it was, was as noon-day compared with what would have been the darkness of his soul under the blight of evil and the bitterness of remorse. The chains that hung about him in his dungeon were but light fetters compared with the chains which would have bound his soul had he yielded to the temptation. Though in a prison, his feet hurt by iron, he was a free man, because his conscience was free and his heart was pure. It requires faith to believe this, but "it is better to suffer any loss, bear any sacrifice, than to sin against God." No fear of consequences should ever drive us to do a wrong thing. Better be hurled down from a high place for doing right than win worldly honor by doing wrong. *Better lose our right hand than lose our purity of soul.* Better rot in prison than be eaten by remorse (Matthew 18:8; Mark 9:43).

MAKING THE BITTER SWEET

Believe it or not, there is something good beyond each distressing experience of life *if we do not permit a wrong reaction and allow bitterness to enter into our own soul.* God is getting us ready for a time of service both here and hereafter that we could never have otherwise. Joseph came through all the painful experiences of his life without becoming hateful or cynical. The noble soul within him rose superior to all the effects of the misfortune and the wrong under which he was suffering. He did not lie down in despair and he was always superior to his conditions and his circumstances because of his faith that agape love is the most powerful force in the universe.

We have reminded you before and, in reminding you, we have reminded ourselves that God is preaching to us through Joseph, telling us that He deals with us *on the very same principles by which He dealt with Joseph.* We have our life's prisons—we have our humiliations—we have our fetters—we have our frustrations. There are times when the chains are upon us; there are times when we, too, are placed under false accusation, wrong, and injustice. *If we are able to keep sweet through all, if our reaction is correct, we too shall find something good on the other side.*

UNHURT BY FETTERS

While the fetters did hurt Joseph's ankles and feet, they did not hurt his soul. He refused to yield to resentment, retaliation, or revenge. He was inwardly triumphant over all the wrongs, injustices, false accusations, and sufferings. He experienced in his period of humiliation a time of growth, of discipline, of training. When he was finally summoned from the prison to sit beside the king, so well was he fitted for greatness that he did not grow dizzy when he stood on this pinnacle of honor and fame.

SUFFERING IN SILENCE
Any one of us may become the innocent victim of calumny. Though blameless, we may have to endure false accusations. As Christians what should we do in such a case? Of course, all cases are not alike. In some instances, vindication may be possible and it may not always be wrong for us to seek it. Sometimes we cannot do even that. In cases like Joseph's, when we cannot free ourselves from false accusations without

bringing dishonor and suffering upon others or when there are circumstances which we cannot explain to the satisfaction of others, then what are we to do? A study of Joseph's experiences teaches us that we are to do as he did—*suffer in silence and in patience. Like Jesus, he left all in God's hands, doing nothing himself to right the wrong.* Because he believed that all things are working together for the good of those who love God, he triumphed over all injustice, self-will, and rebellion.

HIS SOUL WAS UNSTAINED
There is a verse in the 37th Psalm which gives us a lesson and a promise: "Commit thy way unto the Lord; trust also in him; and he shall bring it to pass. And he shall bring forth thy righteousness as the light, and thy judgment as the noonday." Joseph committed his way into the Lord's hands that terrible day when he was falsely accused. He kept his hands off. He was three years under the black cloud of accusations by Potiphar's wife. But then he came forth into the light and there was not a stain upon his soul.

Those were hard years for Joseph, as were all those thirteen years, from the day the boy was sold to the passing caravan till he was summoned by Pharaoh and lifted to honor. But hard as they were, they did not hurt him *because his reactions were right.* That is a wonderful lesson. How often, under mild irritations and pinpricks of criticism and slander we grow vengeful, hard, and cynical and are tempted to say that virtue does not pay. Joseph remained gentle, beautiful, and sweet under all of the trials of those years— under all the wrong, cruelty, heartlessness, injustice,

inhumanity from his brothers, then slavery, degrada-
tion, false accusations, and shame. Some of us can
hardly keep sweet under imaginary slights and the
common frictions and microscopic hurts and griev-
ances. Some of us grow morbid and misanthropic if a
friend omits some simple amenity. Somebody ignores
us, maybe forgets to speak; we feel we are not ap-
preciated. When a friend fails to call when we expected, we grow disenchanted and disillusioned and run
off to get someone to soothe our ego and sympathize
with our self-pity and self-love.

RULERSHIP TRAINING
The noble bearing of Joseph teaches us how to be
superior to all circumstances and conditions, to all
unkind or unjust treatment. *That is the great lesson of life.*
If you are going to resent, resist, and be unforgiving
in every change of social temperature, every variation
of experience, your spirit running up and down like
the mercury in the thermometer with the fluctua-
tions of the atmosphere, you are going to have a sorry
time of it, and in the process may lose eternal rank.
We must aspire to live unaffected by circumstances,
and Joseph has shown us how. Morbidity is sickly
living. Discouragement is not divine. We must be
strong in the grace of God. We must be unconquerable
through Him that loved us. We must put misfortune,
adversities, personal injuries, suffering, and trials
under our feet and use them for stepping stones. We
must conquer ourselves. We must keep the heart
sweet, gentle, brave, strong, loving, forgiving, full of
hope under the worst that the years can bring. Then
when we are suddenly wanted for a great duty we

shall be prepared for it just as Joseph was. *All of this is a part of our training for rulership. It is the opportunity to practice and grow in agape love.*

GROWTH THROUGH ADVERSITY

Today, God uses these principles in training us for high service and for rulership in the *afterwards*. In the case of Joseph there were many, many things which would have made most of us bitter, which would have broken our spirits and caused us to surrender to resentment, but which he overcame by a right reaction. Only a close personal relationship with God made this possible. *Because of this he came through unhurt.* His spirit was still strong and sweet. He was triumphant over all the circumstances that would have made the ordinary person despondent and hopeless. *Only a deep devotional life brought him through without despair.* God is telling us through this experience that if we will take the worst that life can bring, without growing hard and cynical, rebellious and resentful, God has something good in store for us, because love grows only through adversity, through testing.

HEART-SICKENING DELAY

There is much in Joseph's experience that would have made the ordinary person misanthropic. Take for instance the butler: Joseph interpreted the butler's dream and told him that he would soon be restored to his master's favor and asked him to remember him when he was restored to his former position. Doubtless, he hoped that the butler, whom he had befriended, would try to do something to get him out of prison. The butler promised.

Two whole years went by and Joseph was still in

prison. The butler had forgotten, but Joseph did not grow pessimistic even then. He could have said, "Yes, this is the reward that I get for helping somebody." He could have said, "Virtue does not pay. This idea of returning good for evil just doesn't work." He could have grown resentful at this point. He had hoped that the butler, who was in close contact with Pharaoh, would have spoken to him and have had Joseph released. Can you imagine how disappointed he must have felt as the days went by, lengthening into weeks and months and then finally into years, until he realized that he had been forgotten?

Yet he did not grow sullen, unforgiving, or vengeful. How could Joseph, or any other person, retain his inner peace and quietness under these conditions? There is only one answer. *He had to be convinced that Romans 8:28 is true and that almighty love is regulating the universe* (Hebrews 1:3). *Joseph had to believe that "my times are in thy hand"* (Psalm 31:15). Only this faith could have enabled Joseph to keep his sanity and triumph over such deception, perfidy, and foul play. *Believe it or not, this faith is as valid today as it was then.* 4353

SEVEN
IT WAS BETTER
FOR JOSEPH

Strange as it may seem, in the end it was better for Joseph that the butler did forget about him, that the butler did not speak to the king for so long a time. This is what might have occurred: Had the butler made intercession for Joseph at once and had Pharaoh listened to the plea and set Joseph free at that time, Joseph could not have gone back to Potiphar's house. He would probably have been sold away from the city, for he was still Potiphar's slave; or he might have been set free to return to Hebron. *In any case, he would not likely have been available when he was needed to interpret Pharaoh's dream. What then would have been the consequences?*

POSSIBLE OBSCURITY
Dr. Miller says that his career would have ended in obscurity. Perhaps he would never have been heard of again and this charming story would never have been written. Pharaoh's dreams would have had no interpreter. The years of plenty would have come and passed, leaving no storehouses filled for the famine

years which followed. In the terrible distress of those years the family of Jacob, with its holy Seed, might have perished from the earth. The ingratitude of the butler, inexcusable as it was, left Joseph in the prison where he suffered unjustly, *but God was keeping him close at hand until the moment came when he would be needed for work of stupendous importance.* While God's purposes were slowly ripening in the world outside, *Joseph's character also was ripening into strength and self-discipline within the dungeon walls.*

GOD'S CLOCK NEVER SLOW

Notice this remarkable statement by Dr. Miller: "So we see again in the wonderful providence of God how every link of the chain fits into its own place with most delicate precision. Nothing comes a moment too soon. Nothing lags. God's providence is like God's nature. Among the stars there are no haphazard movements. Men calculate transits, eclipses, conjunctions a thousand years ahead and know to the smallest fraction of a second that the calculations will be verified. The sun never rises late. No star sets too early. *So in providence everything comes in its set time. God's clock is never a second slow.*"

Can this be chance? Can nature's perfect adjustments be chance? Can the wonderful beauty and beneficence of providence be chance? A mere endless succession of happy blessed coincidences? Oh, no, there is a God whose hand moves the machinery of the universe, and that God is our Father. *"He [the Son] regulates the universe by the mighty power of his command"* (Hebrews 1:3, *The Living Bible*). "The hands that are pierced do move the wheels of human history and mold the circumstances of individual lives." Nothing is left to pure accident. All things are working together for the good, not only of Joseph, not only of characters in the Bible, but of everyone who loves the Lord. *"There is a heart beating at the center of all things"* (Maclaren). He who has ears to hear cannot but hear it.

Thus in Joseph's life every smallest event was wrought into the final result with perfect adaptation. The inhuman wickedness of his brothers in selling him, the foul lie of Potiphar's wife which sent him to a dungeon, the ingratitude of the butler which left him friendless and forgotten for two years in prison—all these wrongs by others were by the divine touch transmuted into blessings as Joseph kept sweet and free from cynicism, and accepted the severe discipline and training. We need to remember, however, *that everything depended upon his reaction.*

EIGHT
THROUGH THE AGES, ONE ETERNAL PURPOSE RUNS

Some of us may say, "That was all right for Joseph, but it just doesn't work today." Listen to Dr. J. R. Miller, who says, "Shall we suppose that Joseph's life was in God's hands in any exceptional sense? Is there any less of God's providence in our life than there was in the life of that Hebrew lad?" If God's Word is true there is not. "Through the ages one eternal purpose runs." *Unless God's Word is a fake, God deals with the least of us on the very same principle He used with Joseph* (2 Chronicles 19:7; Romans 2:11, 8:28; Ephesians 6:7-9; Colossians 3:23-25). If we will meet the hurts of life, the injustices and the wrongs, in the same spirit Joseph met them, the same results shall be ours. We shall be fitted for high duty and high service as we live with the same faith with which Joseph lived.

Dr. Miller says, "He did not see the providence at the time. Not until afterward did the dark clouds disclose their silver lining or the rough iron fetters reveal themselves as gold." Not until afterward shall we see that our disappointments, hardships, trials, misfortune, and the wrongs done to us by others were all made parts of God's providence toward us. Not until afterward—*but the afterward is sure* if only we firmly and faithfully follow Christ and keep our own hands off.

God works slowly and is never in a hurry because he doesn't need to be. The light which shines from this story of Joseph ought to shine into a great many lives today with its beam of cheer and hope for those who are waiting amid discouraging circumstances. The heart of God is beating and the hand of God is working in each life's experiences. Perhaps the hour for full revelation has not yet come on the dial of the clock of God. Perhaps someone reading this message now finds it impossible to believe that there is anything significant in his life and circumstances. Satan wants everyone to believe this. That thought is inspired by him. It stems from the pit. It is Satan's effort to rob you of initiative and drive you to supine surrender, to total discouragement, and eternal loss. *Do not accept this slander upon God's character. God loves you as fully as He ever loved anyone. He has as wonderful a plan for your life as he had for Joseph's.*

The Word of God teaches that "there is no respect of persons with God" (Romans 2:11; Ephesians 6:9; Colossians 3:24, 25). In this last passage Paul is speaking of slaves. Slaves seem to be the most oppressed and degraded class of all people. Yet because God is the Supreme Ruler and loves everyone equally, *even a slave has as much opportunity for reward, advancement, and honor as anyone else* in the ultimate kingdom. Addressing slaves, he says, "And whatsoever ye do, do it heartily, as to the Lord, and not unto men; Knowing that of the Lord ye shall receive the reward of the inheritance:

for ye serve the Lord Christ. But he that doeth wrong shall receive for the wrong which he hath done: and there is no respect of persons." *Thus the scales of Eternal Justice are so finely tuned and perfectly balanced that even a slave may so serve God as to be equal in eternal rank with the greatest saint. Hallelujah!*

> *Sometime when all life's lessons have been learned,*
>   *And Sun and Stars forevermore have set,*
> *The things which our weak judgments here have spurned,*
>   *The things o'er which we've grieved with lashes wet,*
> *Shall flash before us out of life's dark night,*
>   *As stars shine most in deeper tints of blue.*
> *And we shall see how all God's plans are right,*
>   *And how what seemed reproof was love most true.*

Unknown

A PERSONAL EXPERIENCE

As a young man, just at the threshold of life, I was stricken with a deadly disease, tuberculosis of the chest, abdomen, and lower bowel. All of my hopes, dreams, and plans were dashed. All of my castles, built so high that they pierced the blue of the sky, came tumbling about my ears and lay shattered at my feet. While I was in what was known as "St. Peter's Ward," the ward for terminal patients of the Veteran's Bureau Hospital in Johnson City, Tennessee, and not expected to live, my mother sent me the lines quoted above.

That has been many years ago now. I thought at the time, "That is a beautiful sentiment—if it only could be true." But as I look back over the years which have intervened I can see, perhaps only partially, only dimly, yet I can see with an ever-increasing illumination the truth of those lines. I thought then that it was a good escape psychology but not logical. I thought it was one of those things which is conjured up for the comfort of those who have been frustrated and have no other comfort. I am sorry it took so long for God to teach me this lesson, even partially—*that all God's plans are right, that God's clock of providence is just as accurate as His clock in nature,* and that in truth all things are accurately working for good to them who love the Lord.

In the letter which carried these lines, my mother told me that God had assured her that He was going to heal me of this deadly disease. At that time my faith in the supernatural was so small that I felt pity for my mother's "irrationality." It was more than three years before God was able to illuminate my crass unbelief and surprise me by a miracle that has continued for over fifty-five years. All of my ministry since that time is based upon and is the result of that affliction and my supernatural healing, restoration, and life-long service. I could not have afforded to miss one drop of the distilled hardship, sacrifice, and discipline.

> *Out of the presses of pain*
> *Cometh the soul's best wine.*
> *And the eyes that have shed no rain*
> *Can shed but little shine.*

EVERY LINK IN THE CHAIN NEEDED

In considering the providence of God as revealed in the life of Joseph, we have seen that not one link in the chain could have been spared. We have seen that even though it seemed a cruel thing for Joseph to suffer at the hands of his brothers and at the hands of Potiphar's wife, and then finally at the hand of the butler who forgot him, yet each of these apparent cruelties was a link in the chain of divine providence, *none of which Joseph could have afforded to miss.*

NINE
SUDDEN FULFILLMENT

At last a turning point was reached. When God's work in his life was complete and when historical events were on target, Joseph suddenly came, after years of preparation and training, to a place of high service. The way seemed long from the pit of Dothan to the steps of Egypt's throne. The dreams of the Hebrew boy were long in coming true. The experiences were hard and tended to crush and destroy the young life. Those thirteen years out of the golden prime of life seemed wasted. Yet we should notice that all this time, in all these experiences, God was training the man for his work.

The butler's dream came true in three days. He did not have to wait very long to realize the fulfillment of his dream, but that was because there was not very much of it when it was fulfilled. It took thirteen years for Joseph's dreams to be realized, and that was because his dreams were so magnificent and far-reaching. If a man's work is of small importance, he can be prepared for it in a little while. When he has a great mission to fulfill, it may require a long time to fit him for it.

Although it is difficult not to grow impatient in God's school because of the slow advancement, it may help us to remember that *the longer the time God takes with our training and the harder the discipline, the larger will be life's service when it is finished.* We do not know how much Joseph recognized of the providence of God in those slow years. We do not know how sorely his faith was tested, but I am personally convinced that he had his "ups and downs" too, his times of sore testing. Although he may have had little glimpses of the fact that God was preparing him for something immense, I have no doubt there were many times when Joseph's spirit was very low and his faith painfully tried. There were doubtless many times when he was tempted to grow hard, bitter, and cynical; but, thank God, his hope was unconquerable, his courage unwavering.

"YOU ARE THE WILL OF GOD"
You may be tempted to doubt it, but God is trying to speak to you and me through this experience, telling us that we are no less the object of God's providence than was Joseph. Here is an exciting and thrilling truth. If we really accept our condition as God's appointment, we may read God's will for us clearly in each day's unfolding as if the divine finger wrote it for us clearly in each day's circumstances, as if the divine hand wrote it for us on a sheet of paper under our eye. When we do this we shall cease our restless struggling. We shall no longer fight so hard for our own way, which, because of our fallen condition, is usually the way of our flesh. *If our will is fully yielded we shall see God in everything and everything in God.* Even the

hurts, even the disappointments that could not in themselves be God's will we shall see as links in the chain of exaltation to higher and nobler service. *And they will be, providing our reactions are right.* When we triumph in this way we are growing in agape love and developing character for eternal rank and rulership.

Did you ever stop to think that God's providences are a Bible for you and for each of us? As Oswald Chambers has said, "You are the will of God." That is, you are if you are fully submitted and remain victorious in your reactions. Our perspective is so limited that we cannot see what God is doing, but the providences of God in our lives are His Bible for us, if we are sufficiently meek. "In disappointments, in sorrow, in loss, in the suffering of injuries at the hands of others, in the midst of pain and trial, *to be able to say God is teaching me some new lessons, training me for some new duties, bringing out in me some new beauty of character, that is to accept the providences of God as our Bible"* (Miller).

To those of us who have not discovered Romans 8:28, life is only a mass of tangled and knotted threads, a can of worms, a snarl of crises with neither rhyme nor reason, a series of accidents without meaning. For many of us, life is composed of inscrutable providence and baffling mysteries. *Remember that one incident left out in Joseph's strange career would have broken the chain and spoiled all. So it is in every life.* All the events are necessary to fit us for a place for which God is preparing us both now and in the afterwards, that is, in eternity. If we doubt this, it is because we do not know who we are. We are unaware of our identity.

TEN
GOD USES MOST
ONLY BROKEN MEN

Sometimes the only way God can work real brokenness in us is by our failure. The human spirit is so
immense, so magnificent, so monumental, so rich in
potential that without grace it aspires to be a God. All
self-will is the result of the desire for self-worship, to
be one's own god. *The human spirit is the only spirit in the
universe that was created in the image of God.* Because of this
it has greater potential than angels, archangels, cher-
ubim or seraphim, or any other created being. Because
fallen and infected with the virus that caused Satan's
destruction, the human spirit retains the satanic as-
piration to be equal with deity. *This is why God uses for
His greatest purposes only meek people, people that have been
broken, emptied of themselves, delivered from their unholy ambition to dethrone God.* This is why it has been said that
"whole, unbruised, unbroken men are of little use to
God" (Miller). Because the world worships success,
sometimes the only way God can break us is by
failure.

This may be a surprise to some, but God is more

interested in the worker than the work. *Without the worker, the work is nothing, a cipher. God created the universe for one purpose, people*—people created in His image to prepare for rulership with Him in the ages to come. He is interested in the outer universe only as it relates to His purpose to obtain an eternal companion called the Bride. This is why He is interested in the worker rather than the work. *He will go to any length to produce a man or a woman who will serve His purpose in eternity.* Very few people, even born-again people, understand that eternity is the object and recipient of all that transpires in time. Time is the crucible of eternity.

No one is prepared to rule until he is broken, made pliable, submissive, responsive to God's will and purpose. God cannot use for His purpose unbroken men who are still rebellious. *He will spend a lifetime to bring a man or a woman into real submission.* Sometimes the only way He can do that is by failure. *If necessary, He may allow a work that He has raised up and blessed to fail in order to discipline a successful leader into brokenness.*

RELATIONSHIP RATHER THAN SUCCESS

It is doubtful that a spiritual leader can be used of God in developing selfless character and agape love in others if he has not himself been truly broken, delivered from self-centeredness by a deep work of the Cross.

God must create brokenness in the leader before He can develop it in his followers. The Christian leader who is not truly broken cannot produce this quality in his disciples. One always begets children, both natural and spiritual, in his own image. *Our danger is to worship a successful enterprise, even a spiritual enterprise.*

Oswald Chambers says, "Beware of any work for God which enables you to evade concentration upon God. A great many Christian workers worship their work." In Luke 10:20 Jesus told the disciples not to rejoice in successful service (like the casting out of demons), yet this seems to be the one thing in which many of us rejoice. In Matthew 7:22, 23 Jesus warns against depending upon that kind of power. Many of us have the numerical view—so many souls saved, sanctified, filled with the Spirit, or healed. *Jesus says that relationship with Him is the truly important thing:* "Do not rejoice that the spirits submit to you, but rejoice that your names are written in heaven" (Luke 10:20). *Without relationship all apparently successful works are false.* And relationship is maintained only by a deep devotional life. "Prayer is the only thing Satan cannot handle" (Jack Taylor). This is because prayer is the only thing that releases the power of the Holy Spirit, and the Holy Spirit is the only power that binds and controls Satan. He is the only person who can prevent the answer to God-inspired prayer.

SUCCESS WITHOUT RELATIONSHIP
IS COUNTERFEIT

Any apparent success that arises out of anything but a deep prayer relationship is spurious. This is why God is interested in the worker rather than the work and in relationship rather than success. *Success without relationship is counterfeit.* Success without relationship has no influence in the spirit realm. It will be destroyed in the flame of judgment. *One's effectiveness in the spirit realm is in direct proportion to his relationship, and his relationship is maintained only by time alone with God and His Word.*

Alone with God, the world forbidden,
Alone with God, oh, blest retreat!
Alone with God, and in Him hidden,
To hold with Him communion sweet.

Oatman

When a spiritual leader falls into the trap of worshiping apparent success and fails in his devotional life, God may allow the work to fail in order to discipline the leader and restore the relationship. *The important thing is not the work we may feel we are doing but the relationship we maintain. When relationship is maintained, God's purpose is being accomplished even though visible results may seem lacking.*

Today most of us are enamored with success. We have a success complex. Perhaps you are asking, what is wrong with success? That depends upon your definition. Only God's conception of success is valid. The world's ideal of success is short-lived. "I have seen the wicked in great power, and spreading himself like a green bay tree. Yet he passed away, and lo, he was not: yea, I sought him, but he could not be found" (Psalms 37:35, 36). "Love not the world, neither the things that are in the world. If any man love the world, the love of the Father is not in him. For all that is in the world, the lust of the flesh, and the lust of the eyes, and the pride of life, is not of the Father, but is of the world. And the world passeth away, and the lust thereof: but he that doeth the will of God abideth for ever" (1 John 2:15, 17).

Success that is only temporal is a farce, a deception. God's ideal of success is found in Joshua 1:8: "This book of the law shall not depart out of thy mouth; but thou shalt meditate therein day and night, that thou mayest observe to do according to all that is written therein: for then thou shalt make thy way prosperous, and then thou shalt have good success." *God is the supreme authority on success in the universe.* Only His ideal and principles of success will survive the ravages of time and the crash of worlds. *The only real success is to use earth and its fading sweets as an apprenticeship for learning agape love because that is the qualification for high rank in eternity.*

ELEVEN
MATURITY
REQUIRES TIME

It does not require much thought nor time to draw the plan for a simple building, such as a chicken coop, barn, or common dwelling, but it requires a long time to conceive the plan and draw the blueprint for a skyscraper, a cathedral, or some other magnificent architectural structure. Because God's plans and plots for your life and mine are so magnificent, so far-reaching, and so involved, it requires time for them to mature. The suspense and mystery connected with those plots and plans must be endured for a longer time, if anything great is to be accomplished through us. To change the figure, a mushroom comes up overnight, but it requires a hundred years for an oak to mature.

THE THEOLOGY OF APPARENT FAILURE
We are often mystified at the methods God uses in developing us for a great work and sometimes apparent failure is a part of God's training and discipline. *Strange as it may seem, apparent failure seems to be an instrument*

in God's hands in preparing His people for larger service. Failure!
We never could think of failure as a part of God's plan
for us. The world worships success, and not only the
world but much of the organized church. But for
thirteen years Joseph was an apparent failure so far as
the fulfillment of his dreams was concerned. Visible
success impresses men, but it impresses neither Satan
nor God. Nevertheless we are taught today that
success is the important thing.

*Not many of us believe this theology, but a man may be greater
in failure than in success.* I wonder how many of us are
willing to risk failure in order to have God's best. All
the heroes of faith faced impossible hazards. I imagine
that if we could have lived in Enoch's day, we would
have thought that his life was a fiasco. As far as the
Word reveals, Enoch's public relations apparently
were a fizzle, a flop, a dud. Three hundred years an
apparent dropout. But what a climax marked the end
of those years! Although long gone, for thousands of
years Enoch has been preaching and is still preaching
to the world. Apparent failure was a part of his
preparation and a part of his training.

Look at Abraham and Lot. From Lot's standpoint,
Abraham was a "washout," a faux pas, an utter
failure. Lot was the sensation as the world would
judge. Lot may have been under the influence of the
worldly philosophy of that day which is very similar
to the worldly philosophy of this day. This popular
philosophy counsels, "Promote yourself, be a public
relations expert, polish your image, publicize your
name. You can't accomplish anything unless you are
popular, unless you are in the public eye." Has not this
philosophy invaded the organized church? Lot pitched

his tent toward Sodom, went down there, and was elected mayor.

You can imagine how sorry he felt for Abraham living out there in the desolate heights of Hebron, living a stern, severe life of separation from the world. Lot may have said to Abraham, "Abraham, you can't do much good, living out there like that. *Get yourself a public relations man. Build up your image." Sometimes we may discover that "prayer is where the action is," that it is more important to make prayer our main business than to be a skilled public relations expert.* There came a day when Lot made this discovery. The shadowy kings of the East came in and burned Sodom, and Lot lost everything. Who was it then that came to his rescue? Who was it that saved the day? It was Abraham, living out in the heights of communion with God. It was Abraham, the separated. He maintained divine relationship. While all of us dread failure, it may be a part of God's discipline and training for us. Lot had to learn the hard way.

A CONTEMPORARY FAILURE

Take Noah for instance. Look what a failure Noah was from the viewpoint of his contemporaries. A preacher of righteousness for 120 years. On one side of the fence alone and the whole world on the other. A man standing on principles which no one else, excepting his own family, accepted. What a courageous man he must have been! You and I—well, many of us cave in as soon as we see the way the wind is blowing. We conform. It may be that we have some convictions, but we give them up under pressure. We sell out cheaply. What weak-kneed people we are because we cannot afford to fail!

Suppose Noah had conformed. What do you think would have happened then? What a loss he himself would have suffered! Think of the part Noah played in the new world and in the ushering in of the Messiah. *Sometimes failure is a part of God's discipline and training to prepare for higher service. Failure may be necessary to beat the stiff backbone of self-confidence out of us.* Only then can the supernatural take over.

When everything is going well, you may think you do not need a saint; but when things begin to go the other way, you are going to want somebody to pray for you who has kept himself unspotted from the world. Failure may be a part of God's mysterious plan for your life too. Remember, "Whole, unbruised, unbroken men are of little use to God" (Miller).

JOB'S EXAMPLE

Perhaps Job is the best illustration of this point. In the entire Old Testament there is no greater example of temporary defeat. Only after Job was totally wiped out by failure was he prepared for God's highest and best either for himself or for the world. Only after his new revelation of God enabled him to see himself as abhorrent, did he humble himself in utter brokenness. Only then was he prepared either for time or eternity.

TWELVE
THE ETERNAL DIMENSION
OF TIME

As another example, let us look at Daniel. Think what a failure Daniel appeared to be on his way to that den of lions. Not many of us would have stood firm for principle in the face of such a situation. But Daniel maintained his relationship by his devotional life (Daniel 6:10). Some of us would have said, "Well, a little prudent compromise here is better than to be too rigid and lose my neck, or my position, or spoil my opportunity for advancement." Oh, for men of principle today! God, give us men. I am preaching to myself. Many of us are so wishy-washy. We have so few convictions for which we will suffer. As soon as we see it is going to pinch, our knees give way and we fall all over ourselves to get in line with the prevailing sentiment.

God seldom uses a man like that. God uses men of strong conviction. Practically every man in the Word of God that He used in any important way was a man that was willing to risk failure. A rare modern positive example is the hero of the recent motion picture

Chariots of Fire. It takes courage, I know. Daniel—a failure! Noah—a failure! Enoch—Elijah—Job—all failures! By the world's standards, most of the prophets were failures (Acts 7:52).

"THE EPITOME OF FAILURE"

Then let us come down to the New Testament and think of the Lord Jesus Christ. He lived for those few brief years and then went to a death of shame. The thrust of the wilderness temptation was to take a shortcut to success. Suppose Jesus had worshiped success—where would the world be today? "He saved others; himself he cannot save" (Mark 15:31). That is the epitome of failure. If one is determined to save himself, he cannot save others.

SUCCESS COMPLEX FROM SATAN

Do you know where this spirit that worships success originates? It comes from Satan. He worships success. He is the promoter of the success syndrome. *Satan does not oppose success even in religion if it interferes or prevents relationship, or if it prevents a deep devotional life.* Satan knows that if he can keep us from prayer by whatever means, he is free to operate. *"Prayer is the only thing he cannot handle"* (Jack Taylor). Therefore, he is not opposed to our most grandiose schemes if they become a substitute for prayer. If he can get a leader so involved in activity as to interfere with his prayer life, Satan has won. This is his most successful strategy.

Samuel Chadwick has said, "The one concern of the devil is to keep Christians from praying. He fears nothing from prayerless studies, prayerless work, and prayerless religion. He laughs at our toil, mocks at our wisdom, but trembles when we pray." We say that we are not depending upon our own endowments, abilities, or creative talent. But we deceive ourselves if we are neglecting relationship which is maintained not by general religious activity, but only by a life of prayer.

Some of us are unconsciously under the influence of Satan's ideals. It is difficult for us to die to success. How many gospel workers have compromised their deepest convictions, because they were convinced they could not have success without compromise. We feel that failure is a disgrace. We are convinced that there can be no usefulness apart from success as the world and our peers view it. Most young gospel workers are bitten with this bug. We will use any method short of—well, short of actual open sin many times—in order to achieve apparent success. All of us battle with this temptation. And yet, because an eternal throne is at stake, there is something greater than visible success, and that is the development of high principle, the maturing of holy character. *The flesh may doubt this, but no matter how a man succeeds, if he does not develop lofty, sublime, Godlike character, he has failed both in time and in eternity.* But if he has developed holy character, which is another name for agape love, he has succeeded, no matter how else he has failed. For that is the purpose that God has in mind in all His dealings with us—the development of Godlike character. *Character is the only real success because rank in eternity is governed by it.*

THE PRESENT MOMENT
HAS ETERNAL DIMENSIONS

The study of Joseph teaches us that we are already living in an *eternal dimension* here and now, because our life style, including our attitudes, dispositions, and tempers, in other words our reactions, are leaving a permanent deposit in our character that is affecting our rulership rank in eternity. "Our light affliction, which is but for a moment, is working for us a far more exceeding and eternal weight of glory" (2 Corinthians 4:17). It was while Joseph was in prison that the "iron entered his soul." Without that he would not have been prepared for the throne. This is also a figure for us. It must have been with this conviction that G. Washington Gladden wrote these courageous lines.

> In the bitter waves of woe,
>   Beaten and tossed about
> By the sullen winds that blow
>   From the desolate shores of doubt,
> Where the anchors that faith has cast
>   Are dragging in the gale,
> I am quietly holding fast
>   To the things that cannot fail.
> And fierce though the fiends may fight,
>   And long though the angels hide,
> I know that truth and right
>   Have the universe on their side;
> And that somewhere beyond the stars
>   Is a love that is better than fate.
> When the night unlocks her bars
>   I shall see Him—and I will wait.

THIRTEEN
FAILURE SOMETIMES SERVES BETTER THAN SUCCESS

God is much more interested in what we are than in what we do, in what we become than in what we achieve. If failure works better than success to make us unselfish, considerate, sympathetic, and helpful to others, if it matures us in agape love, then God may permit failure because our eternal promotion is involved. May I repeat that for emphasis? If failure serves better than success to make us unselfish, considerate, sympathetic, and helpful to others, if it matures us in agape love, then God may, in love to us, permit failure.

Holy character is, after all, selflessness—agape love. It was while Joseph was in prison that the iron entered into his soul, the iron of principle, the iron of holy purpose and holy character. *In all that God does with us, in all the puzzling and bewildering vicissitudes of life, His purpose is the development of Christlike character, of pure selflessness, of agape love.* Failure may be a better instrument to achieve that in us than success. Follow the course of a man who has unbroken success and you will find that he is often arrogant, overbearing, cocksure, full of selfishness and inconsideration of others. *If God is going to perfect Christlikeness in you and in me, it may sometimes involve the failure of our ambition, of our plans, of our dreams, of our hopes.* I know it is unwelcome, but if we ask for God's best, then we must be prepared to face the process by which He works it out in our lives.

EVEN SUCCESS IN GOD'S WORK
MAY HINDER GOD'S HIGHEST PURPOSE
Dr. J. R. Miller has said, "The object of all divine culture is to sanctify us and to make us vessels meet for the Master's use. To this high and glorious end, pleasure, gratification and success must oftentimes be sacrificed. This is the true key to all the mysteries of providence. Anything that hinders entire consecration to Christ is working us harm and though it be our tenderest joy, though it be our most cherished ambition, it had better be withheld or taken away. *Nothing should hinder our consecration to the person of Christ alone, and success is often such a hindrance.*" (Emphasis mine.)

Even success in God's work (strange as it may seem) may sometimes absorb the heart's devotion which Christ Himself longs for, and of which He alone is worthy. I know of nothing that hurts the servant of God more than the feeling that he has made a failure in his efforts to glorify God, or failed in his efforts to advance His kingdom. How often ministers and other gospel workers must face this prospect, including the thought that the thing they tried to do to advance the kingdom was a failure; it did not succeed.

I do not know of any sincere gospel worker who has not passed through that death. And yet that very failure may be a part of God's higher purpose to work in him a deeper devotion to the Person of the Lord Jesus Christ and the development of the love that equips for rulership in eternity. How easy it is for one to become possessive of a work that God has entrusted to his care. It is difficult to remain devoted utterly to the Person of the Lord Jesus Christ. *In the midst of acclaim, in the midst of the flush of accomplishment, we are in danger of falling in love with our work more than with Him for whom it is being done.* Then our work, a successful enterprise, a religious venture becomes our unconscious idol and we sacrifice everything to that idol, including people—our loved ones, our colleagues, or anyone else who gets in our way.

DEFEAT MAY SERVE GOD'S PURPOSE
It may be that God will have to smash even the work which He has raised up in order to keep us meek, humble, broken, and devoted altogether to the Person of Christ. When everything is going well, we are in mortal danger of worshiping success—even more than we do the person of the Lord Jesus Christ. Personally, I am afraid of it.

How often we pad our reports! How glowing we make them! How often we tell of the revivals that we hold or the work in which we are engaged in such a way as to reflect credit and glory upon ourselves, instead of glorifying the name of the Lord Jesus Christ. How much self-glory there often is in our accounts of the work that is entrusted to us.

May the Spirit of God search us through and through. May I repeat: even success in God's work may sometimes absorb the heart's devotion for which Christ longs. God may have to remove His favor from a work and allow it to fail in order to produce a higher and a holier character in the worker, thus preparing him for an eternal throne.

> *Defeat may serve as well as victory*
> *To shake the soul and let the glory out.*
> *When the great oak is straining in the wind,*
> *The boughs drink in new beauty, and the trunk*
> *Sends down a deeper root on the windward side.*
> *Only the soul that knows the mighty grief*
> *Can know the mighty rapture. Sorrows come*
> *To stretch out spaces in the heart for joy.*

Streams in the Desert

FOURTEEN
A WORD FROM SPURGEON

Dr. Charles Spurgeon was not unaware of the danger of success. He said,

We have seen many professed Christians make shipwrecks. In some few instances, it has been attributable to overwhelming sorrows, *but in ten cases to one, it has been attributed to prosperity.* Men grow rich and, of course, they do not attend the little chapel they once went to. They might go where the fashionable world worships. *Men grow rich and straightway they refuse to keep to the road of self-denial, which once they so gladly trod.* An insatiable ambition has come over them and they fall, and great is the sorrow which their fall brings to God. But a man in trouble, a man who has failed, see *how he prays. He cannot live now without prayer. See how he reads the Bible now.* He does not care for worldly literature now. He cannot feed on whims and fancies now. *When a man has failed, when he is broken and humiliated, then he sees the vanity of the world and its reward.* He holds the world with a very loose hand. *He wears the world as a loose garment.* Now he becomes heavenly- instead of earthly-minded. The world has lost its attraction for him. (Emphasis mine.)

Spurgeon joins the song writer who has seen the vanity of worldly success:

The things of the world seem so small to me,
Of riches far greater I sing.
When the stars have grown old and the sun has grown cold,
I shall still be a child of the King.

Streams in the Desert

Haven't you found it this way in your own life? When all is well and there is no cloud in the sky, when there are no threatening circumstances and there is no opposition, then you grow careless and neglect your prayer life and your Bible. But when a heavy blow comes, and when the storms of sorrow sweep over your soul, then you fly to the Lord Jesus. Then you go to your knees. Then you go to the Word of God. The magazine and the newspaper lose their attraction for you. The things of this world seem to lose importance, and you see the emptiness and vanity of all the emoluments of a cruel, wicked, deceitful world. Your soul is driven to God.

THE CHRIST ON HIS CROSS?
Mr. Spurgeon says, *"I greatly question whether we grow in purity much, except when we are in the furnace."* How true it is that we have to be driven, rather than drawn to God. This, of course, is by reason of the hardness of our own hearts. You know the furnace is the instrument that is used to refine precious metals, and those metals can

never be refined as long as they are outside the furnace. It is when the metal is in the heat, not when it is lying on the floor outside, or in the hands of the smelter, that it is refined. It must go into the furnace, it must go into the flame, if it is to be purified. And so it is with us in our spiritual growth. It seems that God cannot refine us except by heat. Iron cannot be tempered except by fire.

A village blacksmith said, "When I am tempering a piece of steel, I first heat it, hammer it, and then suddenly plunge it into the bucket of cold water. I very soon find whether it will take temper or go to pieces in the process. When I discover after one or two tests that it is not going to allow itself to be tempered, I throw it on the scrap heap and sell it for a cent a pound when the junk man comes around.

"So I find the Lord tests me, too, by fire and water and heavy blows of His heavy hammer, and if I am not willing to stand the test, or am not going to prove a fit subject for His tempering process, I am afraid He may throw me on the scrap heap."

When the fire is hottest, hold still, for there will be a blessed "afterward"; with Job we may be able to say, "When he hath tried me, I shall come forth as gold" (Job 23:10).

Sainthood springs out of suffering. It takes eleven tons of pressure on a piano to tune it. God will tune you to harmonize with Heaven's keynote if you can stand the strain.

> *Things that hurt and things that mar*
> *Shape the man for perfect praise;*
> *Shock and strain and ruin are*
> *Friendlier than the smiling days.*

GLORIFYING GOD IN THE FIRES

You remember, I am sure, that the prophet said of Israel, "I have chosen thee in the furnace of affliction." We wonder why it is that God must appear so cruel as to choose any of us *in* the furnace of trial. Well, if we are to be refined and purified, God has to allow us to pass through the fire. Do not be deceived, *there is no other way. There is no other method.* God does not have any other way to refine us, just as the smelter has no other way to refine metal. We must pass through the fire. And there is where we are to glorify the Lord. When we yield to the fire's refining and purifying work, that is when we are really glorifying God. God has to permit the searching fires of persecution, misunderstanding, criticism, ostracism, misrepresentation, misinformation, and many other painful things in order to refine and purify us.

> *Pain's furnace heat within me quivers,*
> *God's breath upon the flame doth blow;*
> *And all my heart in anguish shivers*
> *And trembles at the fiery glow;*
> *And yet I whisper, "As God will!"*
> *And in the hottest fire hold still.*
>
> *He comes and lays my heart, all heated,*
> *On the hard anvil, minded so*
> *Into His own fair shape to beat it*
> *With His great hammer, blow on blow;*
> *And yet I whisper, "As God will!"*
> *And at His heaviest blows hold still.*
>
> *He takes my softened heart and beats it;*
> *The sparks fly off at every blow;*
> *He turns it o'er and o'er and heats it,*

And lets it cool, and makes it glow;
And yet I whisper, "As God will!"
And in His mighty hand hold still.

Why should I murmur? for the sorrow
Thus only longer-lived would be;
The end may come and will tomorrow,
When God has done His work in me;
So I say, trusting, "As God will!"
And, trusting to the end, hold still.

Julius Sturm

FIFTEEN

THEREFORE, FAILURE IS SOMETIMES BETTER THAN SUCCESS

Failure may be a part of God's necessary discipline. To change the figure, most of us need the rod. Most of us must have it. Few of us seem to learn obedience except through suffering. We read that even the strong, pure Son of God learned obedience by the things which He suffered (Hebrews 5:8). *Even He, who had no rebellion in His heart, was said to have learned obedience in that way. Thus pain is oftentimes better for us than pleasure.*

> *The cry of man's anguish went up to God,*
> > *"Lord, take away pain:*
> *The shadow that darkens the world thou hast made,*
> > *The close-coiling chain*
> *That strangles the heart, the burden that weighs*
> > *On the wings that would soar,*
> *Lord, take away pain from the world Thou hast made,*
> > *That it love Thee the more."*
> *Then answered the Lord to the cry of His world:*

THE MYSTERY OF GOD'S PROVIDENCE

"Shall I take away pain,
And with it the power of the soul to endure,
Made strong by the strain?
Shall I take away pity, that knits heart to heart,
And sacrifice high?
Will ye lose all your heroes that lift from the fire
White brows to the sky?
Shall I take away love that redeems with a price
And smiles at its loss?
Can you spare from your lives that would climb unto me
The Christ on His Cross?"

Streams in the Desert

GOD USES BOTH SORROW AND LOSS

Loss and gain, sorrow and joy, disaster and deliverance are often better because by a proper reaction to these things holy character is made (Romans 5:3). Faith should know that God's withholdings from us, when He does not give what we ask, may produce richer blessings than opening to us all the treasure houses at whose doors we stand and knock so vehemently.

I am preaching to myself now. I would not have you think that this does not come home to me with as much force as it does to you. It is as necessary that I shall face the application of this truth as it is that you face it. I dare not preach it to you, unless I am willing that God shall hold me responsible for what I say to you and see that it works out in my own life. God alone knows the inner history of the souls of men.

Let us remember that the difficult things that come may be a part of God's discipline to prepare us for larger and greater service, not only here but in glory.

UNFORGIVENESS, A BOOMERANG

With God's permission, Satan is going to see to it that each of us will be the victims of wrong treatment, of injury, injustice, malevolence, misrepresentation, inequity, foul play, and deceit. *No one who wants God's best is immune.* Satan will engineer this in order to turn us against God and blame Him. Satan means it for evil but God means it for good, and He has the wit and wisdom to outsmart Satan and transform his most diabolical schemes into the most sublime good *if and when our reaction is right.* This is one of the most significant lessons of the story of Joseph. He recognized this and was able to forgive his brothers (Genesis 45). Suppose Joseph had sought revenge. *He would have lost the golden opportunity of being a link in the chain of events that ushered in the Messiah.* All unforgiveness acts like a boomerang. That kind of reaction injures the unforgiving person and robs him of untold blessing.

NO SECOND CAUSES

When we understand that there are no second causes operating in the life of a believer and that the God who "regulates the universe by the mighty power of His command" never permits anything to come to one of His children that is not good, *if and when his reaction is correct,* then we can easily forgive all offenses and offenders. When we comprehend that even Satan is under God's control and can do nothing without God's permission, then we see that "our times are in God's hand," not in Satan's. And even our so-called foes are men which are "Thy hand, O Lord," as David said in Psalms 17:14.

One of the most glorious insights in the entire story is revealed in Genesis 45:5, 8. "Now therefore be not

THE MYSTERY OF GOD'S PROVIDENCE

grieved, nor angry with yourselves, that ye sold me hither: for God did send me before you to preserve life. . . . So now it was not you that sent me hither, but God." *Three times in four verses he traces his captivity to God. Joseph was able to see God behind second causes.* Then in Genesis 50:20 he said, "But as for you, ye thought evil against me, but God meant it unto good, to bring to pass, as it is this day, to save many people alive." *This should prove to us that nothing that anyone does to us can harm us when our reaction is right. Right reaction will transform intended evil into good, not once but always in every situation. Romans 8:28 will prove true in all circumstances when we learn to accept everything as from God and allow it to teach us deeper dimensions of agape love.*

> *In a factory building there are wheels and gearings,*
> *There are cranks and pulleys, beltings tight or slack—*
> *Some are whirling swiftly, some are turning slowly,*
> *Some are thrusting forward, some are pulling back;*
> *Some are smooth and silent, some are rough and noisy,*
> *Pounding, rattling, clanking, moving with a jerk;*
> *In a wild confusion in a seeming chaos,*
> *Lifting, pushing, driving—but they do their work.*
> *From the mightiest level to the tiniest pinion,*
> *All things move together for the purpose planned;*
> *And behind the working is a mind controlling,*
> *And a force directing, and a guiding hand.*
>
> *So all things are working for the Lord's beloved;*
> *Some things might be hurtful if alone they stood;*
> *Some might seem to hinder; some might draw us backward;*
> *But they work together, and they work for good.*
> *All the thwarted longings, all the stern denials,*
> *All the contradictions, hard to understand,*

And the force that holds them, speeds them and retards them,
Stops and starts and guides them, is our Father's hand.

Annie Johnson Flint

The story of Joseph illustrates and confirms the truth of Hebrews 1:3: "He [Jesus] regulates the universe by the mighty power of his command" *(The Living Bible). Since this is absolutely true, nothing can go wrong in a universe that He regulates because that universe is serving His purpose.* What comfort, what assurance, what a sense of security for those who love God. The entire universe under the Son's regulation is working together for their good. All born-again lovers of God "have it made," both for time and eternity, because "our times are in His hand" (Psalm 31:15).

DESTINED FOR THE THRONE

Dr. Warren Wiersbe, former pastor of Moody Church, Chicago, Ill., said: *"Destined for the Throne* is the best book I have ever read on the true meaning of prayer in the life of the believer and the church. It puts prayer in the broad perspective of God's eternal purpose, and this is important."

Paul Crouch, founder/president Trinity Broadcasting Network said: *"Destined for the Throne* has meant more to Jan and me than any other book, next to the Bible."

Floyd Nicholson, pastor of Mustard Seed Church, Allendale, New Jersey, said: "In my opinion *Destined for the Throne* ranks next to the Bible in the message it carries to the church."

DON'T WASTE YOUR SORROWS

Dr. Jack R. Taylor, evangelist/author, Fort Worth, Texas, said: "I could not lay this book aside until I had finished reading it. It speaks to the mystery of suffering as no other book I have ever read."

LOVE COVERS

Ras Robinson, editor *Fulness* Magazine, Fort Worth, Texas, wrote: "This volume is a classic in Christian literature. It provides a viable platform for Christian unity. Fellowship should be based upon relationship to Christ, a common parenthood in God, rather than upon a common theology or opinion."

DESTINED TO OVERCOME

This book discovers for us our weapons and the technique of their effective use in spiritual warfare. "Behold I give you authority over all the power of the enemy" (Luke 10:19). Satan works only by bluff and deceit. He has no power except that which we grant him by default.

DESTINED FOR THE CROSS

"The throne of the universe is a cross. The Law of the universe is self-sacrifice." In his Foreword, Dr. Ken Taylor says: "How I wish I had had this book in my early days. How much spiritual suffering it might have saved me." The author adds: "The only people who have genuine authority over Satan are those who choose to stay on the cross, allowing it to deliver them from all self-seeking, self-serving, and self-promotion. The only time that Satan cannot touch us is when we are on the cross."